Lisa D. Hoff

# NEW ORLEANS

## LOUISIANA

## Sightseeing in 88 Pictures.

# NEW ORLEANS — PAST AND PRESENT

On Mardi Gras day in 1699 a small French-Canadian expedition dropped anchor near the mouth of the Mississippi to colonize "La Louisiane." This was the name given to the colony by René-Robert Cavalier, Sieur de La Salle, 17 years earlier when he claimed the mighty river for his king and patron Louis XIV. During the next few years the expedition built posts and fortifications along the river and the Gulf Coast. The beginning of the new colony was stormy; hurricanes, floods, insects, sickness and discontent among the 200 settlers were just a few of the problems with which the young governor, Jean Baptiste Le Moyne, Sieur de Bienville, had to deal.

In 1718 he decided to build a permanent settlement on the site where the river's "beautiful crescent comes closest to the lake." He named the new settlement *La Nouvelle-Orleans* for the Duke of Orleans, who was ruling France for young Louis XV. The earliest settlers, many of whom where French prisoners and convicts, lived in flimsy huts which were inundated or washed away when the river overflowed or when one of the many hurricanes hit. Yet, in spite of all adversity, the city took shape, and the first census taken in 1721 counted 470 people: 145 men, 65 women, 38 children, 29 indentured white servants, and 193 black and Indian slaves. Three times as many people resided in the outskirts of town where ten times as many slaves worked the indigo plantations. In 1721 a group of German immigrants, duped by French agents who promised them land in what is now Arkansas, were invited to settle above New Orleans. These Germans became the colony's most productive, hard-working citizens.

New Orleans lost all stigma of colonial outpost in the 1740s and '50s. The new governor, Marquis de Vaudreuil, arrived at *his new post determined to teach his settlers French sophisti-*

*cation,* courtliness, elegance and the art of lavish entertainment. For 15 years Vaudreuil and his beautiful wife presided over a little Versaille, and New Orleans' balls and soirees became a legend in London, Paris and New York.

Meanwhile, the long-running dispute between France and England over who owned what in America erupted into war. In 1763, when the French and Indian War ended, France had to cede all its territories east of the Mississippi and in Canada to Great Britain. However, New Orleans and the area west of the river were not included in this deal. France had already given New Orleans and the western area to the King of Spain in order to entice Spain to enter the war on the side of the French.

Louisiana Frenchmen opposed the change to Spanish rule. In October, 1768, the first Spanish governor, Don Antonio de Ulloa, was driven from Louisiana in a bloodless coup. Retaliation from the mother country was swift. In July, 1769, General O'Reilly, backed by a Spanish fleet and 2000 soldiers, proclaimed Louisiana a Spanish colony and executed the ringleaders of the rebellion in the Place d'Armes. In spite of this inauspicious beginning, New Orleans prospered during the Spanish rule. *After the two great fires of 1788 and 1794, the ill-built and defenseless French city with muddy streets and low wooden houses, gave* way to a stately Spanish town of 8,000 inhabitants, with a stockade enclosing most of the town and forts at four corners.

The Spanish governors also opened New Orleans to new-comers from all over the world, among them about 5,000 French Canadians from Nova Scotia. These hard-working people, called Acadians or Cajuns, had been expelled some years earlier from their homeland Acadia for refusing to swear allegiance to the Protestant King of England. Most of them settled in the swamps south and west of New Orleans.

During the American Revolution, Spain supported the colonists. The Spanish Governor in New Orleans, Bernard de Galvez, led several successful expeditions against the British and recaptured Baton Rouge, Mobile, Pensacola and West Florida. After the American Revolution, flat-boats, keelboats, canoes, rafts, ferryboats, and crude paddlewheels began to come down the great river with their merchandise. The new agricultural prod-ucts; sugar cane and cotton, were just beginning to make Louisiana planters among the wealthiest people in the New World.

By the end of the 18th century New Orleans had become a major port handling cargo from all over the world. The arrival of white French planters and free people of color, fleeing the successful slave uprising in Saint-Domingue, infused the city with French culture, voodoo religion and fine island food. Free people of color quickly became a distinct and educated caste of New Orleans society. They provided artisans, artists, poets, sculptors and experts in wrought iron lace work.

The beginning of the 19th century saw Louisiana again become a French colony; however, Napoleon soon lost interest in France's foothold in the New World, and, anxious to finance his imminent war

against England, he sold the entire Louisiana colony to the United States for $15 million. The Louisiana Purchase was signed in 1803.

The "Americanization" of New Orleans moved quickly with a new American suburb, an American city hall and an English newspaper and theater. Yet the Creoles stubbornly clung to their French language, their French cuisine, their city hall (the Cabildo), their duels, their cafes and ballrooms and their French theater and newspaper, even their own Civil Code.

In 1812 Louisiana became the 18th state of the Union. The same year the first steamboat came chugging down the Mississippi and was greeted with wonder and excitement by big crowds lining the levee. Furthermore, 1812 brought war against Britain which ended for New Orleans in 1815 with the battle at Chalmette.

The years between the Battle of New Orleans and the Civil War have been described as they city's golden era. By 1820 the population had reached 25,000. During the next 10 years it doubled, and by 1840 New Orleans, with a popula-tion of 102,000, was the third largest city in America. The bustling port was choked with steamboats and vessels of all kind. Wharves, levees and storehouses were packed with goods and raw materials destined for all parts of the world. Two million bales of cotton crossed its wharves annually. The "Queen City of the South" led the nation not only in exports but also in duels fought, in the fre-quency of its epidemics, and in the number of ballrooms and gambling houses.

On January 26, 1861, Louisiana seceded from the Union. Less than four months after secession, a Union fleet blockaded the mouth of the Mississippi River, causing severe economic hardship to the city. In April, 1862, the Union fleet, after sinking most of the Confederate ships, anchored off the wharves of the South's greatest city. Union troops occupied New Orleans and did not leave the city until reconstruction ended 15 years later. By then, Louisiana, the richest state in the antebellum South, was one of the poorest.

The next forty years brought some economic growth to New Orleans. Electric lights were installed, and, by draining the city and the surrounding swamps, the open gutters and cisterns were eliminated, and this ended the devastating epidemics. The 1884 World's Industrial and Cotton Centennial Exposition helped expand trade with Latin America.

By 1910, so many Italian immigrants had arrived in New Orleans that they represented one-third of the population. The French Quarter became known as Little Italy.

In the early twentieth century, a new musical form born in New Orleans was fast becoming the rage in New York, London and Paris. Almost all the early jazz greats were New Orleans musicians: Buddy Bolden, King Oliver, Jelly Roll Morton and Louis Armstrong, to name just a few. In the 1920s and '30s the French Quarter became a gathering place not only for musicians but also for writers, painters and sculptors.

The discovery of oil in the Louisiana tidelands set off an increase of industry around New Orleans and made the city one of the busiest ports in the country.

The construction of the Louisiana Superdome in the 1970s and the 1984 World's Fair have changed the Central Business District and the adjacent Warehouse District dramatically. Modern office buildings, a state-of-the-art convention center, luxurious high-rise hotels, charming apartments and elegant art galleries have replaced once dilapidated warehouses. The new "Arts District" is quickly becoming a Southern SoHo.

Today, the two cities - one two centuries old, a French/Spanish city, the other a modern towering American city - have managed to preserve the old traditions and the *joie de vivre* of New Orleans' French heritage.

Acknowledgements:

**My special thanks are due to:**

Mr. Don Marquis, New Orleans Jazz Club Collection
Mr. Maurice Baxter, Baxter Printing
Mr. and Mrs. Jean-Michel Bock
Dr. Elisabeth Schafer
Longue Vue House and Gardens
The Historic New Orleans Collection
Gallier House Museum, Tulane University
Greater New Orleans Tourist and Convention Commission
New Orleans Pharmacy Museum
Ripley's Believe It or Not!
Mr. and Mrs. Brian Eversole
Mrs. Zeb Mayhew, Sr.
Oak Alley Plantation
San Francisco Plantation

**Photo Credit:**

* Louisiana State Museum (5)
  Anne-Christine Hoff (6c,10,46,47d)
  Jan White Brantley (9)
  Jan White Brantley and Robert S. Brantley (cover)
  Robert S. Brantley (2)
  Historic New Orleans Collection (11)
* Historic New Orleans Collection (18,19)
* Gallier House Museum (13)
* Louisiana Children's Museum (32)
* CAC, Alan Karchmer (33)
* Musee Conti (40)
* Hermann-Grima House (42,43)
  Brian Eversole (48,49)
* New Orleans Museum of Art (53)
* Houmas House Plantation, Ron Calamia (64)

**Art Credit:**

* Charles Gandolfo, Curator Historic Voodoo Museum (44)
  Elisabeth Hoff

* Donation of photograph and artwork is gratefully acknowledged.

# L'HISTOIRE DE LA NOUVELLE-ORLÉANS

Le Mardi gras 1699, une expédition franco-canadienne jeta l'ancre à l'embouchure du fleuve Mississippi pour coloniser "la Louisiane". C'est ainsi que René-Robert Cavalier, Sieur de la Salle, avait nommé la colonie qu'il avait reclamé pour son roi, Louis XIV, en 1682.

Les immigrants construirent des fortifications le long du fleuve et de la côte du golfe du Mexique. Le début de la colonie fut difficile: des ouragans, des inondations, des épidémies et du mécontentement parmi les immigrants ne furent que quelques'uns des problèmes que le jeune gouverneur, Jean Baptiste Le Moyne, Sieur de Bienville, dut résoudre.

En 1718, il décida de construire une colonie permanente là où le "beau croissant du fleuve se rapproche le plus au lac". Il l'appella "la Nouvelle-Orléans" pour le Duc d'Orléans qui règnait en France pour le jeune Louis XV. Ces pionniers, dont beaucoup avaient été des prisonniers, vécurent dans des cases déplorables qui furent noyées chaque fois que le fleuve débordait. Malgré toutes ces difficultés la Nouvelle-Orléans grandit. En 1721, la population comptait 470 hommes, femmes et enfants.

En 1740/50, la Nouvelle-Orléans perdit toute marque de colonie. Le nouveau gouverneur fut déterminé d'enseigner à ses sujets l'élégance et la politesse française, ainsi que la chevalerie avec son code et son étiquette. Pendant 15 ans, le Marquis et la Marquise de Vaudreuil présidèrent à des soirées somptueuses et à des bals élégants, qui devenaient des légendes à Londres, Paris et New York.

En attendant, la question, depuis longtemps disputée entre la France et l'Angleterre, à savoir qui possédait quoi dans le Nouveau Monde, éclata. En 1763, quand la guerre Franco-Indienne finit, la France dut céder toutes ses terres à l'est du Mississippi et au Canada. La Nouvelle-Orléans n'y était pas comprise car la France l'avait déjà donnée au roi d'Espagne.

Les Français de Louisiane s'opposèrent à l'Espagne. En octobre 1768, le premier gouverneur espagnol fut chassé de la colonie dans un coup non-violent. Les représailles ne se firent pas attendre. En juillet 1769, le général O'Reilly arriva avec une flotte espagnole, réclama la Louisiane pour l'Espagne et ordonna de fusiller les rebells sur la place d'Armes. Malgré ce début peu favorable, la Nouvelle-Orléans prospéra sous le règne de l'Espagne. En 1788 et 1794, des incendies détruisirent la plupart des maisons de la cité. La ville élégante de 8.000 habitants qui remplaça les vieilles maisons du style des Antilles avait un charactère espagnol marqué.

Les gouverneurs espagnols invitèrent des immigrants de tous les coins du monde à s'installer en Louisiane.

Ainsi 5.000 Acadiens (Cajuns) du Canada arrivèrent après avoir été chassés par les Anglais de la Nouvelle-Écosse pour refuser de faire acte d'allégeance au roi protestant d'Angleterre. Ces colons laborieux s'installèrent dans les marécages à l'ouest et au sud de la Nouvelle-Orléans.

Pendant la Révolution, l'Espagne supporta les colonistes. Bientôt après, des "flat-boats", des pirogues, des canots et des chalands chargés des marchandises déscendirent le grand fleuve jusqu'à la Nouvelle-Orléans. Des produits nouveaux: la canne à sucre et le coton, commencèrent à amener de vastes fortunes aux planteurs louisianais. Vers la fin du 18e siècle la Nouvelle-Orléans était un port fleurissant.

Des planteurs d'origine française, des gens de couleur libres et des esclaves, fuyants une révolte d'esclaves à Saint-Domingue, arrivèrent en 1791. Ils apportèrent la culture française, la religion vaudou et la cuisine des îles. Les gens de couleur libres devinrent une classe éduquée et artistique de la Nouvelle-Orléans.

Au début du 19e siècle la Louisiane devint de nouveau une colonie française. Bien que Napoléon avait des plans grandioses pour cette colonie, il dut la vendre aux États-Unis pour 15 millions de dollars afin de pouvoir financer la guerre contre l'Angleterre. L'acte de cession de la Louisiane fut signé en 1803.

L'américanisation de la Nouvelle-Orléans s'effectua sans délai. De grandes maisons américaines furent construites au-delà de la rue du canal, un maire américain gouverna de l'Hôtel de ville à Lafayette, et un journal anglais informa les gens des programmes du Théâtre Anglais. Cependant, les créoles maintenaient leurs coûtumes ancestrales, les bals, les duels, la chasse, la langue française, l'aisance à danser le quadrille, les théâtres, même leur code civil.

En 1812, la Louisiane devint le dix-huitième État de l'Union. Le même année le premier steamer s'aventura sur le Mississippi et s'amarra au long du quai de la capital où une foule etonnée l'attendait. En 1812, la guerre avec l'Angleterre éclata et dura jusqu'en 1815. Elle finit pour la Nouvelle-Orléans avec la bataille de Chalmette.

Les années de 1815 jusqu'au début de la Guerre de Sécession étaient des années dorées pour la ville. En 1820, elle comptait 25.000 habitants, ce nombre doubla en dix ans. En 1840, la Nouvelle-Orléans, avec une population de 102.000, était parmi les trois villes les plus grandes des États-Unis. Le port était encombré des steamboats fluviaux et des navires de tout genre. Des balles de coton, des pains d'indigo du delta, la mélasse et le sucre de la Louisiane et de l'Alabama, les farines de blé et de froment de l'Illinois, les barils de boeuf séché de l'Arkansas et les tonneaux de porc salé du Missouri s'entassaient pêle-mêle sur les quais.

Le 26 janvier 1861, la Louisiane sortit de l'Union. Quatre mois plus tard, des navires unionistes bloquèrent l'embouchure du Mississippi et arrêtèrent tout commerce. En avril 1862, quatorze frégates et canonnières remontèrent le fleuve et apparurent face à la cité, après avoir coulé des frégates confédérées. L'orgueilleuse cité se voyait soumise à la loi du Nord. Pendant quinze ans des troupes unionistes occupèrent la cité. La Louisiane, un des états les plus riches dans le Sud du temps Antébellum, devenait le plus pauvre.

Dans les 40 ans qui suivirent, la Nouvelle-Orléans se remit un peu des ravages de la période de Reconstruction. Des lumières électriques furent installées et les marais autour de la cité furent drainés ce qui élimina les épidémies. L'Exposition du Coton et de l'Industrie développa le commerce avec l'Amérique du Sud.

Au début du vingtième siècle une nouvelle forme du musique qui était née à la Nouvelle-Orléans faisait fureur à Paris, Londres et à New York. Presque tous les géants du jazz venaient de la Nouvelle-Orléans: Buddy Bolden, King Oliver, Jelly Roll Morton et Louis Armstrong, pour en nommer quelques uns. En 1920/30, le Vieux Carré était le centre intellectuel pour musiciens, auteurs et artistes.

La découverte du pétrole dans les marécages de la Louisiane mit en marche une nouvelle industrie. Le port de la Nouvelle-Orléans est aujourd'hui le port le plus fréquenté du Sud des États-Unis.

La construction du Superdome dans les années 1970 et l'Exposition Mondiale en 1984 ont changé le district central des affaires et le quartier voisin. Des bureaux grattes-ciel, un centre de congrès ultra moderne, des appartements luxurieux et des galeries élégantes ont remplacé des entrepôts dilapidés.

Aujourd'hui les deux cités — l'une vieille et franco/espagnole, l'autre moderne et américaine — ont réussi à préserver les traditions ancestrales et la joie de vivre de la Nouvelle-Orléans d'autrefois.

# DIE GESCHICHTE DER STADT NEW ORLEANS

Am Faschingsdienstag des Jahres 1699 ankerte eine Gruppe von französisch-kanadischen Schiffen nahe der Mündung des Mississippi, um von dort aus „La Louisiane" zu kolonisieren. So hatte Rene-Robert Cavalier, Sieur de La Salle, das Gebiet genannt, das er 17 Jahre früher für seinen König, Ludwig XIV., in Besitz genommen hatte.

Während der nächsten Jahre errichtete die Expedition einige Außenposten und Festungen entlang des Flusses und der Golfküste. Der Anfang der neuen Kolonie war schwierig: Orkane, Überschwemmungen, Ungeziefer, Krankheiten und Unzufriedenheit unter den 200 Ansiedlern waren nur einige der Probleme, mit denen sich der junge Gouverneur, Jean Baptiste Le Moyne, Sieur de la Bienville, befassen mußte.

1718 beschloß er eine dauerhafte Siedlung an der Stelle des Flusses zu errichten, wo der „schöne Halbmond sich am meisten dem See nähert". Die neue Siedlung wurde „La Nouvelle-Orleans" genannt, zu Ehren des Herzogs von Orleans, der Frankreich für Ludwig XV. regierte. Die ersten Ansiedler, von denen viele französische Sträflinge waren, wohnten in armseligen Hütten, die ständig überschwemmt oder weggespült wurden. Trotz aller Schwierigkeiten wuchs die Stadt. Die erste Volkszählung im Jahre 1721 ergab 470 Einwohner, davon waren 145 Männer, 65 Frauen, 38 Kinder, 29 verdungene Arbeiter und 193 Sklaven.

Zwischen 1740 und 1750 verlor New Orleans die Merkmale eines Kolonialpostens. Der neue Gouverneur, Marquis de Vaudreuil, brachte seinen Ansiedlern französische Eleganz und Lebensart und die Kunst, großartige Empfänge zu geben, bei. 15 Jahre lang herrschten der Gouverneur und seine schöne Frau über ein kleines Versaille. Die Empfänge und Parties waren in Paris, New York und London berühmt.

In der Zwischenzeit entwickelte sich der Streit zwischen England und Frankreich um die amerikanischen Besitzungen zu einem vollen Kriege. Mit dem Friedensschluß im Jahre 1763 verlor Frankreich alle seine Besitzungen im Osten des Mississippi und in Kanada an Großbritannien. New Orleans und die westlichen Gebiete waren jedoch nicht im Friedensvertrag genannt, da diese schon vorher an den König von Spanien abgetreten worden waren.

Die Franzosen in Louisiana weigerten sich, spanische Untertanen zu werden. Im Jahre 1768 wurde der erste spanische Gouverneur in einem gewaltlosen Coup aus Louisiana vertrieben. Die Bestrafung vom Mutterlande ließ nicht lange auf sich warten. Im Juli 1769 erklärte General O'Reilly, unterstützt von einer spanischen Flotte und 2000 Soldaten, Louisiana zu einer spanischen Besitzung und ließ die Führer des Aufstandes auf dem Place d'Armes hinrichten. Trotz dieses nicht vielversprechenden Anfanges gedieh New Orleans unter der spanischen Herrschaft. Nachdem Brände 1788 und 1794 fast alle Häuser vernichtet hatten, ließ der spanische Gouverneur die Stadt schöner als zuvor im spanisch/karibischen Stil wiederaufbauen.

Die spanischen Gouverneure hießen Ansiedler aus aller Welt willkommen, unter anderem 5.000 französische Kanadier aus Neuschottland. Diese fleißigen „Cajuns" waren aus ihrem Heimatlande, Akadia, vertrieben worden, nachdem sie sich geweigert hatten, dem protestantischen König von England den Untertaneneid zu leisten. Die meisten siedelten sich in den Sümpfen südlich und westlich von New Orleans an.

Spanien unterstützte die Kolonisten während der amerikanischen Revolution, und innerhalb kurzer Zeit erschienen amerikanische Flöße, Kanus, Flachboote, Kielboote und plumpe Raddampfer beladen mit Waren im Hafen von New Orleans. Die neuen landwirtschaftlichen Produkte, Zuckerrohr und Baumwolle, waren in der ganzen Welt gefragt, und viele der Mississippi Pflanzer wurden reiche Plantagenbesitzer.

Mit dem Ende des 18. Jahrhunderts gewann der Hafen von New Orleans immer mehr an Bedeutung. Französische Plantagenbesitzer und freie Farbige, die vor einem Sklavenaufstand in Sant-Domingue flüchteten, kamen nach New Orleans und brachten ihre französische Kultur, Voodoo Religion und gute karibische Küche mit. Die freien

Farbigen bildeten sehr bald eine eigene kultivierte und künstlerisch begabte Schicht der Bevölkerung.

Zu Anfang des 19. Jahrhunderts wurde Louisiana wieder eine französische Kolonie. Allerdings verlor Napoleon bald jegliches Interesse an seinem Stützpunkt in der Neuen Welt, und da er ständig Geld für seine Kriege brauchte, verkaufte er die Kolonie um 15 Millionen Dollar an die amerikanische Regierung. Der Ankauf Louisiana's erfolgte 1803.

Die Amerikanisierung von New Orleans ging sehr schnell vor sich. Eine neue amerikanische Vorstadt mit eigener Stadthalle, eigener englischer Zeitung und englischem Theater bildete sich flußaufwärts von der Canal Strasse. Die Creolen klammerten sich unterdessen verzweifelt an ihre französische Sprache, ihre französische Küche, ihre Duelle, ihre Stadthalle (Cabildo), ihre Kaffeehäuser und Bälle und ihre französischen Theater, sie behielten sogar ihre eigene französische Zivilgesetzgebung bei.

1812 wurde Louisiana der 18. Staat der Vereinigten Staaten. Im selben Jahr ankerte, zum Erstaunen der Bevölkerung, das erste Dampfschiff im Hafen von New Orleans. 1812 führte England wieder einmal Krieg gegen Frankreich. Dieser Krieg endete für New Orleans mit der Schlacht von Chalmette 1815.

Die Jahre zwischen der Schlacht von New Orleans und dem Bürgerkriege wurden oft als die Goldenen Jahre der Stadt bezeichnet. 1820 war die Bevölkerung auf 25.000 angewachsen. Während der nächsten zehn Jahre verdoppelte sie sich, und im Jahre 1840 war New Orleans die drittgrößte Stadt Amerikas.

Der Hafen war voll von Dampfern und Schiffen aller Art. Kais, Piers, Dämme und Lagerhäuser waren vollgestopft mit Gütern und Rohmaterialien, die in alle Welt verschickt wurden.

Am 26. Januar 1861 trat Louisiana aus den Vereinigten Staaten aus. Kaum vier Monate später blockierte die Flotte der Union die Mündung des Mississippi und brachte die Wirtschaft New Orleans' zum Stillstand. Im April 1862 ankerte die Flotte der Union, nachdem sie mehrere föderalistische Kriegsschiffe versenkt hatte, am Kai gegenüber von Jackson Square. Die Besetzung der Stadt dauerte 15 Jahre bis zum Ende der Rekonstruktionszeit. Louisiana, der reichste Staat des Antebellum Südens, wurde in diesen 15 Jahren einer der ärmsten Staaten.

Die nächsten vierzig Jahre brachten etwas wirtschaftlichen Aufschwung. Elektrisches Licht wurde installiert, und durch die Trockenlegung der Stadt und der umliegenden Sümpfe gelang es endlich, der vielen Seuchen Herr zu werden. Die Weltausstellung für Industrie und Baumwolle von 1884 half den Exporthandel nach Südamerika auszudehnen.

Anfang des 20. Jahrhunderts wurde eine neue Art von Musik, die in New Orleans ihren Ursprung hatte, große Mode in New York, London und Paris. Fast alle frühen Jazzgrößen waren aus New Orleans: Buddy Bolden, King Oliver, Jelly Roll Morton und Louis Armstrong, um nur einige zu nennen. In den Zwanziger— und Dreißiger Jahren wurde das Französische Viertel zum Treffpunkt nicht nur für Musiker, sondern auch für Schriftsteller, Maler und Bildhauer.

Mit der Entdeckung von Öl in den Überschwemmungsgebieten von Louisiana begann die industrielle Entwicklung und mit ihr der Ausbau des Hafens. Heute ist der Hafen von New Orleans einer der größten Häfen in Amerika.

Der Geschäftsbezirk und das anschließende Lagerviertel wurden durch den Bau des Louisiana Superdomes und durch die Weltausstellung von 1984 sehr aufgewertet. Moderne Bürogebäude, Kongreßzentren, Luxushotels und elegante Wohnungen und Kunstgalerien ersetzen die heruntergewirtschafteten Lagerhallen.

Beiden Städten von New Orleans — die eine 200 Jahre alt und französisch/spanisch im Stil, die andere eine moderne amerikanische Stadt mit hohen Wolkenkratzern — ist es gelungen, die alten Traditionen und die „joie de vivre" der französischen Vorfahren beizubehalten.

**Jackson Square.** Until the 1850s Jackson Square was named Place d'Armes and served as town center, parade ground and place of execution. St. Louis Cathedral is the oldest active cathedral in the United States. The first church dates back to 1724-1727. This building is a gift of Don Andres Almonester y Roxas and was built from 1789-1794 after the original cathedral burned to the ground.

**Statue of General Andrew Jackson,** victorious leader of the battle of New Orleans in the war of 1812 against the British under General Sir Pakenham.

**The Presbytere** and the Cabildo, Jackson Square. Both are Spanish colonial buildings and were built shortly after the great fire of 1788. To the left is the Cabildo named for the Spanish council or city hall. In 1803 the Louisiana Purchase documents were signed on the second floor of the Cabildo. The Presbytere was originally designed to house the priests of the cathedral. Today both are part of the Louisiana State Museum Complex.

**The Pontalba Apartments** on either side of Jackson Square were built in 1850/51 by Micaela Almonester, Baroness de Pontalba, daughter of the legendary Don Andrés Almonester. The baroness also designed Jackson Square.

**The 1850s House,** 523 St. Ann Str., open to the public, is a model of one of the townhouses as it looked for the first residents during the most prosperous time of New Orleans' history.

Around Jackson Square.

**Moon Walk.** This promenade along the levee is named for Moon Landrieu, mayor of the city in the 1970s. In front is the mighty Mississippi as it curves around New Orleans, giving the city the name of the Crescent City. The river flows to the left for another 100 miles until it meets with the Gulf of Mexico.

**French Market.**

In the background is the streetcar named Desire which did actually run between Desire Street in the Faubourg Marigny and Canal Street. Tennessee Williams lived at 632 St. Peter Street when he wrote "A Streetcar Named Desire."

**Louisiana State Museum,** Old U.S. Mint, 400 Esplanade Ave. Jazz Exhibit; the only museum of its kind, this exhibit shows the history of New Orleans jazz through instruments, pictures, sound and videos. Shown in this picture are young Louis Armstrong's first bugle and cornet. The Mardi Gras exhibit includes floats, costumes and crowns used by different Mardi Gras Krewes (organizations).

10

LA COUVENT DES R. URSULINES — 1732 — BROUTIN

**Old Ursuline Convent,** 1112 Chartres Street, built 1734-1752. The convent is the oldest French colonial building in the Mississippi Valley as this reproduction of the ink drawing by the architect shows. The church was added in 1845. The Ursuline Sisters arrived in New Orleans in 1727, to attend to the sick and the orphans, and to start a free school for girls.

**Beauregard - Keyes House,** 1113 Chartres Street, open to the public. Built in 1826, this mansion was the temporary home of Confederate war hero General Pierre Gustave Toutant Beauregard who ordered the first shots of the Civil War fired onto the Union troops at Fort Sumter, South Carolina. Novelist Frances Parkinson Keyes restored the house and garden.

**Gallier House Museum,** 1118-1132 Royal Street, open to the public. Built by New Orleans architect James Gallier, Jr., in 1857 as his personal residence.

Most of the New Orleans houses were rebuilt during the last decade of the Spanish rule after the great fires of 1788 and 1794. This accounts for the Spanish architecture of the French Quarter.

**Madame John's Legacy,** 632 Dumaine Street. Built in the late 1790s, this house is the exact replica of a 1726 house. The wooden structure, built in the West Indies-style gives you an idea of what New Orleans might have looked like before the great fires. The name was adapted from a short story by George Washington Cable about a "free woman of color" who was the mistress of a Frenchman and inherited the house upon his death.

**Quadroon Ballroom,** 717 New Orleans Street. According to legend, quadroon balls were elegant affairs to which free women of color, famous for their beauty and charm, would come, escorted by their mothers, to meet young Frenchmen. In 1881, an order of black nuns purchased the Quadroon Ballroom.

**LaBranche House,** 700 Royal Street, built in the 1830s, has some of the finest examples of ironwork on its balconies.

**Historic New Orleans Collection, Williams Residence,** 533 Royal Street, open to the public. The collection, located within a complex of historic houses, is a research center for state and local history. The Williams residence, a 19th century townhouse, reflects the elegant 20th century lifestyle of the collection's founders.

**Historic New Orleans Collection, Louisiana History Galleries,** 533 Royal Street. Original maps, prints, paintings, documents and memorabilia take you through New Orleans' and Louisiana's history and culture. Shown here is an 18th century portrait of New Orleans' founder Jean-Baptiste le Moyne, Sieur de Bienville.

20

**Napoleon House,** 500 Chartres Street. A longtime favorite haunt for local writers and artists, the house was built between 1797 and 1814 and reportedly offered to Napoleon Bonaparte as sanctuary. Unfortunately Napoleon died before the schooner "Seraphine," one of the fastest ships in the world, could sail for St. Helena to rescue him.

**New Orleans Pharmacy Museum,** 514 Chartres Street. This building was the apothecary shop and residence of America's first licensed pharmacist, Louis J. Dufilho, in the 1820s. However, the practice of herbal medicine in New Orleans goes back to the 1730s and to sister Xavier of the Ursuline order who was the first woman pharmacist in America.

**Le Petit Theatre,** 616 St. Peter Street. The building was erected in 1789 and has been a community theater since 1916. The first theater in New Orleans was opened in the 1780s. Between 1825 and the Civil War, New Orleans boasted three major theaters with opera productions staged in English, French and Italian. Next to the theater is Le Petit Salon, a typical Creole home which became a ladies' literary club.

**Pirates Alley.** The little garden behind the cathedral has been the site of many duels. Until the Civil War there was scarcely a man in public life who had not fought at least one duel. The rules for duels were carefully defined in the Code Duello and no young Creole's education was complete without the knowledge of the Code and without attending one of the many academies for sword, rapier or pistol training. William Faulkner wrote his first novel "Soldier's Pay" while he lived in house Nr. 624.

New Orleans Patios.

**Jax Brewery.** A former brewery, now a shopping and entertainment complex.

**Canal Street,** seen from the Top of the Mart. In the 1830s New Orleans became a "divided city" and Canal Street was the dividing line that separated the Creole part of the city from the Anglo community above Canal Street. The seat of the American government was in the city of Lafayette, while the French Creoles had their city government on Jackson Square.

**Aquarium of the Americas.** Lets you see a Caribbean Reef, an Amazon Rainforest, the inhabitants of the Gulf of Mexico, and a bayou of the Mississippi Delta.

New Orleans seen from Algiers.

**Riverwalk Marketplace,** an old warehouse district that has been transformed into a half-mile marketplace with over 140 specialty shops, restaurants and cafes. The 1984 World's Fair was held on this tract of land.

The soap film tent poster reads:

**SOAP FILM TENTS**

1. Dip string into soap, holding ends of all four sticks together.

2. Take sticks out of soap, holding ends together.

3. Stretch strings apart carefully. You have made a soap film tent.

4. Hold sticks at different levels. What shapes can you make?

**Louisiana Children's Museum,** 428 Julia Street. Exhibits encourage children to learn by touching, exploring and by getting involved in a fun and entertaining way.

**The Contemporary Arts Center,** 900 Camp Street, features art exhibitions as well as theatrical, dance and musical performances. The artworks shown are from the Robert Cary Tannen REPROspective which was part of the inaugural exhibition at the CAC's reopening in October 1990.

**Gallier Hall,** Charles Street. Built in 1850 by local architect James Gallier, Jr., was the seat of the American city government during the antebellum years.

Skyline of the Central Business District (CBD).

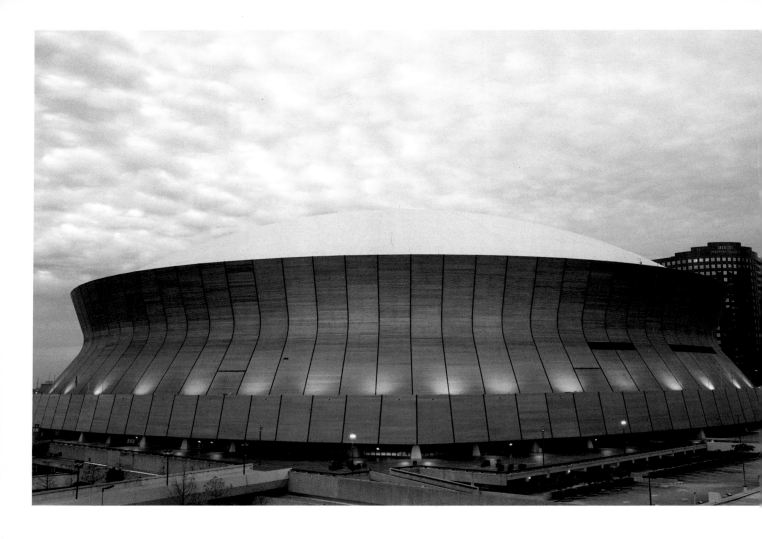

**Louisiana Superdome.**

Joan of Arc
Krewes of Poydras
Ocean Song
Governor Galvez
John McDonogh

**St. Louis Cemetery,** 400 Basin Street. The oldest cemetery in New Orleans, originally located outside the city limits. New Orleans was built below sea level, it was therefore difficult to bury bodies underground without having the coffin float to the surface after the first hard rain. The most famous grave is the tomb of Marie Laveau, the Voodoo Queen, who died in 1881. The red X's that mark her tombstone are wishes that were made known to the voodoo queen by her devotees.

**Our Lady of Guadaloupe Church,** 411 N. Rampart St., built in 1826 and known for its large St. Jude shrine. The church served as burial chapel during the yellow fever epidemics that struck New Orleans on average every third year.

**Musée Conti Wax Museum,** 917 Conti Street, tells the story of New Orleans in chronological order. This scene shows the arrival of the "Casket Girls," orphaned young French women who volunteered to make the New World the land of their future. They were the charges of the Ursuline nuns until their marriages. Each girl carried her trousseau in a basket.

**Ripley's Believe It or Not!** 501 Bourbon/St. Louis Street. Among the many unusual items displayed here is an exhibit of New Orleans Mardi Gras Indians. Tradition has it that people of mixed, black and Indian blood formed the first tribe in the 1880s. Mardi Gras Indians, wearing intricate hand-made costumes, sing as they march and dance, with second liners singing back responses.

**Hermann-Grima House,** 820 St. Louis Street, open to the public. Built in 1831, this is one of the best preserved examples of American architecture in the Quarter. Has a restored private stable and a Creole kitchen where cooking demonstrations are held every Thursday from October through May.

Samuel Hermann came to the country from Germany, and became a wealthy commission merchant in New Orleans. In 1844 the house was purchased by Judge Felix Grima whose family lived there for five generations.

**New Orleans Historic Voodoo Museum,** 724 Dumaine St. Voodoo was imported to New Orleans in 1791 by refugees from Saint-Domingue. Voodoo is a mixture of different African religions, cults of the West Indies, witchcraft and Roman Catholic liturgy. Although outlawed, its rituals were performed on St. John's Eve along Bayou St. John. The powerful Voodoo queen, Marie Laveau, presided also over tamer versions of voodoo ceremonies in Congo Square (now Louis Armstrong Park).

**Lafitte's Blacksmith Shop,** 941 Bourbon Street, a favorite local bar. The "Terror of the Gulf," Jean Lafitte, arrived in New Orleans in 1806, and opened a blacksmith shop from which he planned his raids against Spanish vessels and slave ships. The seized merchandise was then sold at stores from Royal Street to Galveston.

Bourbon Street.

**Mardi Gras.** There has never been a time when New Orleans did not love a parade, from the day in 1827 when young Creoles back from Paris staged the first costumed parade, to the more than sixty parades which float, dance and march through the streets during Mardi Gras now.

The flambeaux carriers traditionally light the way of night parades. The 'doubloons' thrown to the onlookers show the krewe's coat of arms and the parade theme of the year.

Garden District.

**Audubon Zoo,** 6500 Magazine St., is one of the top American zoos, with over 1500 animals and an award-winning Louisiana swamp exhibit.

**Pitot House,** 1440 Moss Street, open to the public. Built in 1799, the Pitot House is one of the few West Indies-style houses which lined Bayou St. John in the early 1800s. The Pitot House was restored and moved to its present location to mark the 1708 site of the first French settlement in the New Orleans area.

**New Orleans Museum of Art,** City Park. This portrait of Estelle Musson Degas was painted by Edgar Degas in New Orleans in 1872.

**City Park,** celebrating the centennial of its founding, boasts the largest collection of mature live oaks anywhere, a Botanical Garden, an antique carousel, tennis, fishing, boating, golf and a children's fairy tale theme park.

Lake Pontchartrain.

**Longue Vue House and Gardens,** 8 Bamboo Road, open to the public. This city estate, surrounded by eight acres of beautiful gardens and fountains is decorated with its original furnishings of English and American antiques. It was designed and built between 1939 and 1942 for Mr. and Mrs. Edgar B. Stern.

**Chalmette National Historic Park** includes the site of the Battle of New Orleans. This battle has been called "The Battle that Missed the War" because news that a peace treaty had been signed did not reach America until after Old Hickory and his hastily assembled army of Kentucky sharpshooters, pirates, slaves, planters, freeman, Indians and Creole dandees defeated the British redcoats on January 8, 1815.

**Barataria,** 8,600 acres of Louisiana's coastal wetlands, including freshwater marshes, swamps and hardwood forests.

**Destrehan Plantation,** built in 1787, is the oldest plantation home left intact in the lower Mississippi Valley. Robin de Logny contracted with a free man of color, Charles Pacquet, for the house and outbuildings. This West Indies-style house is typical of the homes built by the earliest planters in the region. European and early American antique furnishings.

**San Francisco,** completed in 1856, is perhaps the most ornate of all Louisiana plantation homes. The architecture of the manor is Creole French in design, but numerous structural anachronisms have caused it to be called "Steamboat Gothic" because of its resemblance to a Mississippi River Boat.

**Oak Alley Plantation,** the 28 gnarled oak trees that give Oak Alley its name were planted in the early 1700s. The house, probably the most famous plantation house in Louisiana, dates from 1839. Spared during the Civil War the house was sold several times till Mr. and Mrs. Andrew Stuart rescued the house from further deterioration in 1925, and pioneered the trend toward restoration of other plantations along River Road.

**Nottoway Plantation,** the largest plantation home in the South, is known as the "American Castle." This Greek Revival and Italianate mansion was built in 1857 and boasts 64 rooms. The white ballroom is renowned for its hand-carved cypress Corinthian columns, crystal chandeliers and white marble fireplace mantels.

**Tezcuco Plantation Home** was completed in 1855. This spacious Creole cottage was designed by James Gallier, Jr. a well-known New Orleans architect. It is elegantly furnished with many fine antiques and artworks.

**Houmas House Plantation** is named after the Houmas Indians. This Greek Revival Mansion was built in 1840 by a transplanted South Carolinian, Col. John Smith Preston, who had come to Louisiana to take over the properties of his father-in-law, General Wade Hampton. The traditional Louisiana-style was used in the construction, but there are many traces reminiscent of the Carolinas. On either side of the house are hexagonal garconnieres for bachelor sons or for travelers who were put up for the night.

# ニューオーリンズ ―― 過去と現在

1699年のマルディグラの日、フランス系カナダ人の小遠征隊がミシシッピ川の河口近くに錨を下ろし「ラ・ルイジアン」に入植した。この植民地の名称は、これに先立つこと17年前にシュール・ド・ラサール、ルネ・ロベール・カバリエが、パトロンである国王ルイ14世のために偉大なるミシシッピ川の所有権を宣言した際に名付けたものである。

その後2～3年間にわたり、ラ・ルイジアンの入植者たちはミシシッピ川及びメキシコ湾岸に沿って駐屯地や砦を築いて行った。入植当初の生活は厳しく、若くして総督となったシュール・ド・ビヤンビル、ジャン・バブティスト・ル・モインは、ハリケーン、洪水、虫害、病に加えて、200名に上る入植者からの不満等の問題に対処しなければならなかった。

1718年、同総督はミシシッピ川の「美しい三日月形の曲線が湖に最も近付く」地点を永住地とし、そこに築いた集落を、当時幼いルイ15世に代わってフランスを治めていたオルレアン公に因んで「ラ・ヌーベル・オルレアン」と名付けた。初代の入植者の多くはフランスの囚人・罪人で、粗末な小屋に住み、ミシシッピ川の氾濫や頻繁なハリケーン襲来のたびに家屋の浸水や流失に悩まされた。しかし数々の苦難にもかかわらず町は発展を続け、1721年の人口調査では、男性145人、女性65人、子供38人、白人の年季契約奉公人29人、黒人及びインディアンの奴隷193人の計470人を数えるまでになった。

1740年代から50年代にかけて、ニューオーリンズは辺境の植民地の汚名を返上した。新総督として赴任したマルキ・ド・ボードレーは、入植者たちにフランス式の洗練された素養と優雅な振舞い、そして贅沢なもてなしのマナーを教えた。ボードレーとその美しい夫人は15年間にわたってこの小ベルサイユに君臨し、ニューオーリンズの舞踏会や夜会は、ロンドン、パリ、ニューヨークでも評判になるほどだった。

一方で、フランスと英国は、米国における領土をめぐって長期にわたる論争を続けていたが、ついに戦争となり、フレンチ・インディアン戦争が幕を閉じた1763年、フランスはミシシッピ川以東

及びカナダの全領土を英国に割譲することを余儀なくされた。しかし、ニューオーリンズ及びミシシッピ川以西の土地は、すでにフランスからスペイン国王に譲渡されていたため、この協定には含まれていない。

ルイジアナのフランス人は、スペインの統治に反抗した。1768年、初代のスペイン人総督ドン・アントニオ・デ・ユロアは、無血クーデターでルイジアナを追放された。しかしスペインの報復は迅速で、1769年スペイン艦隊と2千人の軍隊を従えたオライリー将軍がルイジアナをスペイン植民地とする宣言をし、反乱の首謀者らをプラス・ダームの広場で処刑した。このように始めは不吉な影がさしたが、スペイン統治の下でニューオーリンズは繁栄した。ぬかるみの道と木造の低い家並みの続く、防御施設もない粗末なフランス植民地は、1788年と1794年の二度の大火の後、ほぼ全周に砦柵を備え四隅には砦を配した堂々たるスペイン風の町に変身し、人口も8千人に達した。

また代々のスペイン人総督は、世界中からニューオーリンズに集まる移民を歓迎し、特にカナダ南東部のノバ・スコシアからは約5千人のフランス系カナダ人が移住してきた。彼らはアケイディアン（アカディア人）またはケイジャンと呼ばれる勤勉な人たちで、プロテスタントの英国王に忠誠を誓うことを拒否したために故郷のアカディアを追放された人たちだった。彼らの多くはニューオーリンズの南あるいは西の沼沢地に住みついた。

米国独立戦争では、スペインは植民地側を支援した。戦争が終わると、平底船・カヌー・いかだ舟・フェリー・外輪船などが商品を積んでミシシッピ川を下ってくるようになった。そしてルイジアナの農園主たちは、新しい農産物であるサトウキビと綿の栽培で、新世界でも最も裕福な階層の仲間入りをするようになる。

18世紀末には、ニューオーリンズは世界中から集まる貨物を扱う主要港湾都市となっていた。また、白系フランス人の農園主や、サンドミング島の奴隷反乱を成功させて脱出してきた有色自由人らが移住してきたため、フランス文化、ブーズー教、島の料理なども流入した。有色自由人は、まもなくニューオーリンズの社会

で独特な、教養ある階級を形成するようになった。

19世紀初頭、ルイジアナは再びフランス植民地となったが、ナポレオンは、まもなく新世界に足場を築くことに興味を失い、英国との開戦に備えて資金を作るために、ルイジアナ植民地を1500万ドルで米国に売却した。これが1803年のルイジアナ購入である。

ニューオーリンズは急速に「米国化」され、米国色の濃い郊外住宅地が新しく発展し、米国風の市役所ができ、さらに英字新聞や英語による劇場などもできた。しかし一方で、フランス系のクリオール人たちは、フランス語を話し、フランス料理や「カビルド（市役所）」、決闘の習慣、カフェ、ダンス場、フランス語の新聞・劇場などの仏文化を頑固に守り、民法までも独自のものを採用していた。

1812年ルイジアナは合衆国の18番目の州となった。この年、初めて蒸気船がミシシッピ川を下ってニューオーリンズを訪れ、堤防を埋め尽くした群衆から熱狂的な歓迎を受けた。さらに1812年は米英戦争開始の年でもあり、ニューオーリンズにおける戦いは、1815年のシャルメットの戦いで米軍の勝利に終わった。

ニューオーリンズの戦いから南北戦争開始までの期間は、ニューオーリンズの黄金時代と言われる。同市の人口は1820年には2万5千人に達し、それに続く10年間でさらに倍増、そして1840年には10万2千人に達して、ニューオーリンズは全米第3位の大都市に成長する。港は蒸気船その他の船舶で混雑し、波止場や堤防、倉庫などには世界各地へ向かう製品や原材料があふれた。ニューオーリンズの波止場を通過する綿花の量は年間200万梱を超えたという。

1861年1月26日ルイジアナ州は連邦から分離した。そのわずか4カ月後、連邦軍（北軍）の艦隊がミシシッピ河口を封鎖してニューオーリンズに大きな経済的打撃を与えた。1862年4月には北軍艦隊が南部連合軍艦隊をほとんど壊滅させて、南部最大の都市ニューオーリンズの沖に停泊した。以後ニューオーリンズは、15年後に再建時代が終わるまで北軍の占領下に置かれ、その間に、戦前南部で最も裕福な州であったルイジアナは、南部の貧困州に転落するのである。

その後の40年間でニューオーリンズは、ある程度の経済復興を遂げた。町に電気が入り、また市内及び周辺の沼地を排水して開渠や溜池をなくしたため、それまで蔓延していた流行病を食い止めることができた。また1884年に開催された世界産業綿花百周年記念博覧会は、ラテン・アメリカ諸国との貿易振興に役立った。

20世紀初頭には、ニューオーリンズで新しく生まれたジャズ音楽が、ニューヨーク、ロンドン、パリなどの大都市で熱狂的に迎えられつつあった。バディ・ボールデン、キング・オリバー、ジェリー・ロール・モートン、ルイ・アームストロングなど初期のジャズ名演奏家は、ほとんどニューオーリンズ出身者で占められている。1920～30年代のフレンチ・クォーターは、ミュージシャンだけでなく作家、画家、彫刻家など芸術家のたまり場となった。

ルイジアナ州の領土水域で石油が発見されると、ニューオーリンズ周辺への産業進出が盛んになり、ニューオーリンズ港は全米でも最も入港船舶数の多い港湾の一つとなった。

1970年に建設されたスーパードームと1984年のニューオーリンズ世界博覧会は、市の中央商業地区や隣接する倉庫地区の様相を大きく変え、荒れ果てた倉庫に代わって、モダンなオフィス・ビルや会議センター、贅沢な高層ホテル、小ぎれいなアパート、シックな画廊などが建ち並んだ。

今日のニューオーリンズは、フランスとスペインの文化に彩られた200年の歴史を持つ町と、近代アメリカの高層都市の二つの顔を持ち、「生の喜び」を謳歌するフランスの伝統を大切に保存したユニークな町となっている。

# Index — New Orleans

**LEGEND:**  Interesting and fun for children of all ages.

 Access for handicapped people.

![partial] Partial access and/or with assistance.

## Tour #1: INNER FRENCH QUARTER
### *(walking tour)*

**Page**

1    St. Louis Cathedral ![partial]
Tel.: 525-9585
Hours: Tours daily 9-5
Admission: Free

3    The Presbytere and the Cabildo ![handicap]
751 and 701 Chartres Street
Louisiana State Museum
Tel.: 568-6968
Hours: Wed.-Sun. 10-5
Admission: Yes

5    The Historic 1850 House, Lower Pontalba
Louisiana State Museum
523 St. Ann Street
Tel.: 568-6968
Hours: Wed.-Sun. 10-3, tours on the hour
Admission: Yes

9    The Old U.S. Mint, Louisiana State Museum
400 Esplanade Ave. ![handicap]
Tel.: 568-6968
Hours: Wed.-Sat. 10-5
Admission: Yes

**Page**

12    Beauregard - Keyes House
1113 Chartres Street
Tel.: 523-7257
Hours: Mon.-Sat. 10-3
Admission: Yes

13    Gallier House Museum
1118-1132 Royal Street
Tel.: 523-6722
Hours: Mon.-Sat. 10-4:30
Admission: Yes

18, 19    Louisiana History Galleries ![partial]
Williams Residence
533 Royal Street
Tel.: 523-4662
Hours: Tues.-Sat. 10-5, tours at 10, 11, 2 & 3
Admission: Yes

22    New Orleans Pharmacy Museum ![partial]
514 Chartres Street
Tel.: 524-9077
Hours: Tues.-Sat. 11-5
Admission: Yes

*You can combine Tour #2 by taking Riverfront Streetcar between observation deck and Moonwalk to Foot of Canal Street/Aquarium, or by taking French Quarter bus at Decatur Street/St. Peter via Vieux Carre and CBD to Canal Street.*

# Tour #2: CANAL STREET, ARTS DISTRICT, CENTRAL BUSINESS DISTRICT (CBD)
## (walking tour and/or CBD Shuttle & St. Charles Streetcar)

**Page**

27    Top of the Mart ♿
2 Canal Street
Tel.: 525-2185
Hours: Daily 9-5
Admission: Yes

28    Aquarium of the Americas ♿ 🧒
1 Canal Street and Woldenberg Park
Tel.: 861-2537
Hours: Daily 9:30-6, Thurs. & Fri. 9:30-8
Admission: Yes

30    Riverwalk Marketplace ♿ 🧒
at Poydras, Canal and Julia Streets
Tel.: 522-1555
Hours: Mon.-Thurs. 10-9, Fri.-Sat. 10-10, Sun. 11-7

Exit at Convention Center (Julia Street)

32    Louisiana Children's Museum ♿ 🧒
428 Julia Street
Tel.: 523-1357
Hours: Tues.-Sat. 9:30-4:30
Admission: Yes

**Page**

Confederate Museum (not shown)
929 Camp Street
Tel.: 523-4522
Hours: Mon.-Sat. 10-4
Admission: Yes

33    Contemporary Arts Center ♿
900 Camp Street
Tel.: 523-1216
Hours: Tues.-Sun. 10-5
Admission: Yes

36    Louisiana Superdome ♿ 🧒
Sugar Bowl Drive
Tel.: 587-3808
Hours: Tours daily, 10, 12, 2 & 4
Admission: Yes

---

# Tour #3: OUTER FRENCH QUARTER
## (walking tour)

*I suggest you take the St. Louis Nr. 1 Cemetery tour by US Park Service. Tour starts every day at 9:30 a.m. at 916 N. Peter Street (French Market). Tel.: 589-2636. Reservation necessary. Length of tour, 90 minutes. If you walk in cemetery on your own, use caution.*

**Page**

38    St. Louis Cemetery Nr. 1 ♿
400 Basin Street
Hours: Weekdays 8-4:30, Sun. & Holidays 8-4
Admission: Free

**Page**

39    Our Lady of Guadaloupe Church
411 N Rampart Street
Tel.: 525-1551
Hours: Daily 6:30-6:30
Admission: Free

## Tour #4: GARDEN DISTRICT
### (streetcar tour, return by cruise ship)

To begin tour, board the St. Charles Streetcar at the corner of Canal Street and Corondelet. Streetcars run 24 hours daily, about every 10 minutes 7 a.m. - 8 p.m., every half hour 8 p.m. - midnight, then every hour. Cost: 80 cents (exact change). The Garden District begins at Jackson Avenue. Most of the district is located in the next five blocks on the left; however, you can see beautiful mansions on either side of St. Charles Avenue.

Exit at Audubon Park (stop #36). Either walk across to the zoo (about 25 minutes) or wait for free Zoo Shuttle (every 15 minutes).

Return downtown (Canal Street Dock/Aquarium) by cruise boat (Tel.: 586-8777). Departs from Audubon Landing (across the levee from the CRUISE EXIT of the zoo) at 11 a.m., 1, 3 and 5 p.m.

## Tour #5: BAYOU ST. JOHN, LAKE PONTCHARTRAIN, METAIRIE
### (by car)

**Page**

*When you exit City Park turn left onto Wisner Blvd. (becomes Beauregard Dr.) which ends to the right into Lakeshore Drive. Right on Robert E. Lee then left into Pontchartrain Blvd., which becomes I-10. Exit Metairie Rd. Turn right. Go 0.6 mi.; turn left onto Bamboo Road.*

---

## Tours #6 & #7:
# CHALMETTE, BARATARIA UNITS OF JEAN LAFITTE NATIONAL HISTORICAL PARK
### (by car)

---

## Tour #8: PLANTATIONS
*(The complete tour is for two days. You can combine it with swamp tour.)*

*Exit Ormond. Turn right onto River Road. Go 20 miles.*

60 **San Francisco**
River Road, Garyville
Tel.: 535-2341
Hours: Daily 10-4
Admission: Yes

*Exit San Francisco. Turn right. Go 7 miles to the Lutcher/Vacherie ferry (every 15 minutes, $1.00 per car). Cross river. Turn right on Great River Road (Hwy. 18). Go 5.9 miles.*

61 **Oak Alley Plantation**
3645 Highway 18, Vacherie
Tel.: 265-2151
Hours: Daily 9-5:30 (9-5 Nov.-Feb.)
Admission: Yes
B & B, restaurant

*Exit Oak Alley. Turn left on Great River Road (Hwy. 18). Go 16 miles to Sunshine Bridge. Turn left onto Hwy. 70 W. Go 17 miles on Hwy. 70; then Hwy. 1 to entrance.*

62 **Nottoway Plantation**
Hwy. 1, White Castle
Tel.: 545-2730
Hours: Daily 9-5
Admission: Yes
B & B, restaurant

*Exit Nottoway and return to Hwy. 70 and Sunshine Bridge, first exit after bridge turn right onto River Road/Hwy. 44, go 1.2 miles.*

63 **Tezcuco Plantation**
3138 Highway 44, Darrow
Tel.: 562-3929
Hours: Daily 10-5 (10-4 Nov.-Feb.)
Admission: Yes
B & B

*Exit Tezcuco Plantation and turn right on River Road. Go 1.6 miles; turn left onto Hwy. 942. Go 0.5 miles.*

64 **Houmas House Plantation**
40136 Hwy. 942, Darrow
Tel.: 473-7841
Hours: Daily 10-5 (10-4 Nov.-Jan.)
Admission: Yes

*To return to New Orleans: Return to Hwy. 70 and Sunshine Bridge eastside. Turn left onto Hwy. 70 (5 miles). Right at Hwy. 22 (1 mile) then onto I-10 (47 miles to New Orleans).*

*If you would like to tour the plantations for one day only, you can either tour the first four plantations (pages 59-61 including Ormond) or the four plantations from pages 61-64. Take I-10 W. to exit LA Hwy. 22 (47 miles). Turn left onto Hwy. 22 then left onto Hwy. 70. Before Sunshine Bridge exit and turn right onto River Road. Follow directions to Tezcuco and Houmas. Return to Hwy. 70, cross bridge and follow directions to Nottoway. Return to Sunshine Bridge, before bridge turn right onto Hwy. 18 to Oak Alley.*

# BOOKS BY CITIES IN COLOR, INC.

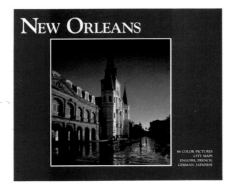

WASHINGTON
SAVANNAH
NEW YORK
*To be published in 1992*

*Also Available:*
Vienna, Austria,
Rio de Janeiro, Brazil

**Cities in Color, Inc.**
**Lisa D. Hoff**
Tel: 404 255-1185 • Fax: 404 252-7218